Whispers from within …

Shuvendu Patnaik

*The photograph of owl in cover page is by
S. Devarajan. It was a two and half foot owl
that looked steadily at him while being
photographed, as if it wanted to impart its
wisdom in stoic silence.*

This book is dedicated to Stewart School,
the school where my learning began.

A wise owl sat in an oak,
The more he heard, the less he spoke;
The less he spoke, the more he heard;
Why aren't we all like that wise old bird?

Edward Thomas

Contents

Foreword

Shuvendu and I go back more than 50 years as freshers and wing-mates at IIT Kharagpur. Over and above that we also happen to be classmates.

It is fortunate we have kept in touch as individuals and as families over the decades. On one of those WhatsApp days, he sent me a couple of his profound insights in just a few brief sentences, which he does on and off. But that day it struck me he should compile them all into a book!

We talked, discussed, and mulled over it. A decision was made. Then onwards he kept sending me a few pages every day. We went back and forth on some, with great progress. Before we knew it, the content was complete. We hit upon a title that looked appropriate. We thought about the cover and got an apt one too from a photograph I had taken some time back in the wild.

He wanted to add some explanation to his insights, but we decided to leave it to readers to discover them or interpret in whatever way they perceive it. Everything just flowed into place, and so very quickly.

I sincerely wish that Whispers from within… is heard by many across the globe to think afresh and set their minds look at life quite differently.

S. Devarajan
Bengaluru

Preface

Since childhood I have been drawn towards a study of the hidden side of things. My study took me to the teachings of Jiddu Krishnamurti that transformed the way I have looked at life.

These are my personal notes. They would have remained as notes had it not been for S. Devarajan, a classmate from my engineering days at IIT Kharagpur who insisted on publishing them, with sound practical guidance and a wonderful philosophic advice.

This book would not have happened without encouragement and support of S. Ravishankar, a schoolmate from Stewart School, who painstakingly reviewed every word with remarkable insight.

The book is organised in four chapters with different topics. This is only for reading convenience and mental separation. The book can be read in any random order. The importance of breaking continuity, not only for this book but also in every aspect of life, is covered in later topics.

Introduction

Life speaks. Sometimes loudly, sometimes softly, sometimes in whispers. It is telling us all the time, but so very silently we can barely hear what it says. There is this breeze of life that tells us something different, something new, all the time. If we do not pay attention, they get louder and build up into a storm.

One cannot ask the whispers, what they are, why they are. One cannot agree or disagree with them. They do not explain themselves. You are too small for me, they will say. There are whispers from within, we can only hear in silence. They are very faint, ready to fade away and die. Unless the mind is very quiet and not buzzing with thought, nothing can be heard. Thinking breaks the silence and the whisper is lost in the cacophony of the mind, never to come back again.

I have tried to capture some of them. The words are few, because not everything is audible. I could have made them louder, but then my interpretation might creep in to pollute and corrupt them. When one listens without arguing or seeking explanations, a fresh aroma begins to spread. That aroma, if you are sensitive and can sense it, carry the truth of life.

The words are unimportant. They are my words. They have little value. It is the space between the words, the blanks, that perhaps speak. If you can create empty space in your mind, you may meet the whispers.

Reflections

*Reflections on life is thought looking at itself
through a mirror.*

REFLECTIONS

Life speaks if one cares to reflect. Pause to reflect over how the day has gone by, just for a few moments before sleep. You may come upon striking insights.

Do not strain yourself to recollect everything. That will make you miserable.

One need not try to remember them. They sink into the mind, ready to arise when needed.

Art of speaking

We speak to communicate our thoughts. Listeners attach it to what they already know, to comprehend the thought.

Thinking clearly before speaking, measuring every word before speaking and a clear diction, improves its quality.

Quality alone is not all. It is the silence between two words that carry messages. Pauses bring life and clarity even to jumbled words and thoughts.

Effective discussions

Dominance in discussions force suboptimal agreements. Personalities often clash bringing disagreements. Energy is lost.

Discussions are effective when participants become a group of nobodies by refusing to steer discussions, with far greater interest to watch themselves while speaking and listening.

That ends psychological distances, ending friction, conserving energy, and quickly arriving at far better outcomes.

Dreams

Why do we dream? Not the nightmares from overeating, but ordinary dreams.

Sleep is a period of rest for our body and mind. But we have subtle bodies that chatter away their content even in sleep to become dreams.

Contents are not gathered if we are attentive when awake. Body and mind can then rest in sleep without dreams.

Prophetic dreams

Contents in our subtle body continue to rattle even in sleep, bringing dreams.

Some contents can be subtle, heralding the future. They result in prophetic dreams when the mind is unusually quiet during sleep.

While awake, the same future can be visible if one is very attentive, and perhaps with far greater clarity than any prophetic dream.

Shower your baby with love

The most powerful communication happens in silence.

Mind-to-mind communication can have unimaginable effect, and feelings of love deliver unimaginable energy.

A newborn has a free mind. Tender thought-feelings of parents touch the baby's psyche instantly, modifying it remarkably. Not a word or gesture is needed. Keep heavy emotions at a distance and shower your baby with love.

Nurturing the young

Parents often drive children with their expectations, wanting them to achieve and become winners in life.

A black crow cannot become a white swan. Yet the crow is unique and intelligent.

No teaching is higher than teaching to accept, observe, and cherish life. Children can flower uniquely when free and shine out naturally in life.

Two facets of education

There are two facets of education.

One is technical education covering book-knowledge and skill-acquisition. It is self-oriented resulting in competition, therefore division and conflict.

The other kind covers human values of togetherness, self-sacrifice, and love. This cannot be learnt from books but needed for an undivided global society. It is sad this education is barely recognised and imparted.

Origin of oppression

Oppression prevents life from flowering in freedom.

Children ingrain values from unspoken psychological signals of parents. "Do this, don't do that" despite all its good intent, is psychological oppression. It constricts a child's mind into obeying and psychological dependence.

Children grow up wearing a cloak of oppression, unknowingly spreading oppression in later life, resulting in a stifled society.

Music

Music is the rhythm of life. It is born from the heart; its melody can be heard from within.

Music expresses itself in colours, which psychics often see. It is a colour language, the language of Gods. A musician lives in harmony with nature.

Musicians are very sensitive to sound, therefore intelligent, as there is great intelligence in music.

Mathematics in nature

Mathematics is a song of numbers, resplendent with beats and tunes, singing the patterns in nature.

Some patterns are captured by thought to become mathematical theories. But thought can never capture every pattern. Mystics sense some of them but are unable to express.

What isn't a pattern in nature is nonexistent, for mathematics is limited by the expression of nature.

Ideas and Reality

Knowledge is ideas put together by thought. Thoughts belong to the past. They can never contain the entire reality of the present, even if accepted as complete and true.

Reality lives in the moving present. Unlike ideas, it is never static.

Reality cannot be gathered or communicated. It becomes stirring and profound with the flowering of intelligence.

Contradictions contain truth

We often come across crossroads and wonder whether this or that.

Is there God or no God? Does time exist or not? Is existence an illusion or reality?

Truth hides in false and false in truth. Figuring them out is only wasting intellectual energy. Contradictions are statements of truth, and the ability to see that is intelligence.

Why do we read?

Reading brings us knowledge for practical life. Its usefulness ends there.

Knowledge soon becomes an impediment, conditioning the mind, making one think along its pattern. It creates a conditioned thinker.

Reading may lead one to learn about its limitations. The wise abandon books to go beyond. So, reading can serve as an enabler to go beyond, for psychological flowering.

Study and cultural activities

Study is a self-centred activity. One gathers knowledge for oneself, but deep learning rarely happens.

Cultural activities are social activities. They build bonds and create togetherness. They unite.

If study is food for the mind, cultural activity is food for the soul. They teach much more than study, through the harmony of relationship.

Artificial intelligence

Enormous advances in artificial intelligence and robotics are frightening. Will machines rule our lives in future?

Artificial intelligence however advanced will remain entirely physical. Emotional and spiritual intelligence can never be created artificially.

Life will continue, perhaps with far greater physical ease amidst destructive intelligence but protective counter-intelligence, as has always happened in history.

Questions

We ask questions to know and learn. Do answers bring learning?

Every answer is judged, the mind rejecting what lies beyond the known. Answers can never bring what we have never known.

Only an indolent mind asks questions, for answer lies in the question if one looks carefully. Observation can cleanse our mind from both questions and answers.

Can knowledge bring wisdom?

Knowledge is content. As it can only be gathered, it belongs to the past, always stale.

Wisdom is a quality of the mind. It cannot be gathered. It is always fresh, operating in the ever-changing present.

The stale can never become fresh; content can never become quality. Knowledge, however vast and deep, can never bring wisdom.

Spirituality

Spirituality is a journey into the science governing nature and all life in it. It demystifies the supernatural by discovering the immutable laws of nature.

It is a journey of observation, unaccompanied by beliefs, knowledge or thought.

Spiritual life means living not in theological theories and beliefs, but in harmony with the fundamental forces of nature.

Theology and science

The universe is a sediment of an all-pervading energy. Theology concerns itself with the energy, calling it God. Scientists study the sediments to discover the laws of nature.

Theology uses the instrument of faith and worship. Science uses intellect and mathematics.

It is the instrument that matters. Both have limitations. Can we not go beyond them all?

Beyond physics

While mathematics expresses the patterns of nature, physics justifies them. If mathematics is king, physics is its minister.

Neither the minister nor the king can ever know the entire kingdom.

What lies beyond is inconceivable and vast. It can never be discovered, for physics ends where thoughts end. Ending of thought brings awareness. One may stumble upon what lies beyond.

Integrity

Integrity is harmony in our thoughts, words and deeds. Whatever is not, is pretense.

Any external effort to create harmony results in pretense. Harmony so created, soon falls apart.

Integrity comes into being naturally when we end pretense. Moreover, energy is not lost. Integrity is goodness, a natural flowering of what we really are.

Discipline

Discipline is not conformance to any dogma, pattern, behaviour or thought imposed by self or by authorities.

It is an outcome of discrimination between the right and wrong, between the more and less important, even between love and affection.

Discipline is intelligent and fearless living in the present.

Self-development

Self-development is a desire for betterment, a dissatisfaction of what we are. It drains energy and breeds discontent while we chase a projected future.

Can we live life wholly in the present with reality as our partner, and not in plans and dreams?

That will bring out the hidden potential in us, while we cherish the fullness of life.

Charity

Charity, as commonly understood, is not charity but an act of selfishness hidden beneath a cloak of philanthropy. The very thought is self-oriented.

When giving happens as an act of compassion, it is instantaneous and free from thought and selfishness. One will strain to even remember he has given.

That is true charity.

Forgiving

Forgiving is a noble act, perhaps the noblest. But what do we forgive? The person, the act, or just our own thought about it?

Thought ends completely when one meets the wrong with love and compassion.

There is no space for thought to arise, and no residue to forgive.

Appraiser is the appraised

An appraiser often sits at a pedestal giving verdicts.

Appraisals then become outcomes of distances created by the appraiser, creating still greater distances that prevent mutual development and organisation growth.

Appraisals become meaningful when the appraiser descends from the pedestal to completely end the distance, upon recognising that appraisals are just his own mirror.

A religious mind

A religious mind is awake and observing, living in the present. It has no desire for knowledge and gathers no belief.

Religions are centres of fear, seeking conformance, telling us what to do.

A religious mind is never a prisoner of any religion. It is a scientific mind, always alert and free.

Austerity

Austerity is careful and intense observation without any denial and therefore without loss of energy. It is an outcome of intelligence that brings about this discipline.

There is tenderness and freedom when austerity is born from intelligence.

Austerity is never self-imposed. That would be harsh and cruel for our body.

Depression and its cure

Depression is a medical condition that sets in when the channel in which thoughts habitually operate dries up creating sediments.

Medicinal intervention makes it worse. It drugs the mind, making it insensitive.

Only companionship and love can take one out of the gloom into joy and rekindle charm in life.

Sexual thoughts

"I have frequent sexual thoughts," he said. "I cannot rid myself of them."

Should we battle sexual thoughts? That only strengthens them, and we lose energy.

Can we accept it as a loving brother and watch it tenderly? Habits change in the silence of observation.

Blindness

Blindness is when our sight has failed us, not just our eyesight.

Our sight fails us when our mind fails us, and we become psychologically blind.

Our mind fails us when it is cluttered with knowledge, convictions, and beliefs. There is little space left in the mind for thought to move about in freedom.

Psychological memory

Memories are often wrapped in a layer of emotional association, called psychological memory. We tend to remember them much more than facts.

They result in tendencies and biases. We carry them as an ever-growing burden until we die.

Psychological memories weigh down our mind, cloud thinking, and wear away the brain. They are harbingers of sorrows and suffering.

Remaining youthful with age

We become senior citizens with age. Senility sets in, making us miserable and pitiable.

Psychological ageing often accompanies physical ageing, as life experiences make the mind hard. The tenderness of youth withers away.

Physical ageing may happen, but we can remain youthful by dying to our psychological memories. The brain remains sharp, and senility doesn't set in.

Success is in doing what we love

We all have different parameters for success. It means different things for different people.

Success is not what you imagine it to be. That is a great illusion of life.

True success is in doing what you love to do, which is also your knowledge. The yardstick for measuring it becomes immaterial.

A monk lives in illusion

A monk surrenders worldly life, often ceremoniously.

Monk is an image created by the mind. This image separates itself from another image called worldly life. The monk then lives in the illusion of its self-created image, with lofty goals.

A real monk is one who can see and end all images. Only images need abandonment, not worldly life.

Who am I?

I am my mind.

My mind has its content of memories, and I associate myself with them. But I am not the content gathered by me.

My intelligence manifests as the container that decides what it can gather. My mind is an outcome of that intelligence, and that is who I am.

Gratitude and grace

Gratitude is an emotion of thankfulness. It takes a selfless form when not directed at someone but towards life in general to become grace.

Living in heartfelt gratitude irrespective of our circumstances, is the highest form of living.

Gratitude when expressed towards an individual carries a taint, instantly descending from its lofty heights to become an instrument of barter.

Esoteric Knowledge

Knowledge is the nectar of life.

Real knowledge is to know the extent of one's ignorance.

Confucius

ESOTERIC KNOWLEDGE

Esoteric knowledge is about the hidden side of life, as known to sages. I had the benefit of studying them from rare esoteric books since childhood, guided by an enlightened person.

I have neither accepted nor rejected esoteric knowledge, but sense truth and wisdom in them. I am writing about some of them, but in my own words and with added insight.

Knowledge is needed for living. Esoteric knowledge, like any other knowledge, is as much true or untrue. The difference is, esoteric knowledge is not imparted in schools or accepted by science and society. So they are not widely known. Rationalists may brand them as figments of imagination and delusions, but they are not so for those who have acquired them in their own way.

Much of this knowledge is contained in theological ideas, ancient glyphs and symbols, and understood by students of esoteric literature and occultism. However, their true meaning is lost in interpretations in exoteric literature.

The topics in this chapter are presented after stripping them of their theological halo.

Worlds of nature

Nature is not just our physical environment. There are several degrees of subtlety, known together as the worlds of nature.

There is an emotional environment, a thought environment, and many more. We live in ignorance of them, blundering and wondering why life is so harsh.

Subtle intelligence is needed to live in harmony with the worlds of nature.

Extra-terrestrial life

Occultism emphasises the existence of extra-terrestrial life in the solar system with irrefutable evidence, postulating several Schemes of Evolution, even naming them.

The Venus Scheme is said to be the most evolved, having produced Mighty Intelligences.

Let us be concerned about ourselves, not about them. Our intelligence is too limited to comprehend their life or study them.

Triple Logos

Nature expresses itself as a Trinity of metaphysical super-principles, the Triple Logos.

They are Brahma, Vishnu and Shiva in Hinduism; Father, Son and Holy Ghost in Christianity; Osiris, Isis and Horus in Egyptian; Amitabha, Manjushri and Avalokitesvara in Buddhism; Taulac, Fan and Mollac of the Druids; and so on.

Esoterically, they stand for Possibility, Ideation and Actualisation.

The nameless

The nameless is the other shore. Some call it the *Paramatman*. That cannot be because *Paramatman* is a part of knowledge, an idea.

The river of knowledge separates the shores. The shore yonder is beyond knowledge and time.

We cannot know it when we arrive as we would have become the shore itself.

Cosmic energy

Is there such a thing called cosmic energy?

If there is, thought cannot know it, for it must be beyond thought. So it is only an idea, a hypothesis, created by thought.

Thoughts must end, and all ideas have to be buried. Cosmic energy, if there is, can only be contained in an ending of thoughts and ideas.

Why temples are powerful

Ancient and much visited temples become centres of concentrated emotional energy, poured in by countless worshippers over hundreds of years.

It is this artificially created emotional energy centre and not god, that gives powerful results, while it binds worshippers to the gross emotional realm.

The same deity housed elsewhere and less visited, will never have such power.

Limitation in idol worship

Idol worship creates elemental deities that become centres of emotional energy, mirroring back the qualities poured into them through worship.

They have a tendency to drag the mind into emotional grossness, not freeing it to rise beyond into subtlety.

People believe that worship imbues qualities of enshrined gods. That never happens as devotion binds one in its chains.

Why idol worship is forbidden

Idol worship makes the mind emotionally dull. Some religions forbid it.

The occult reason is now history. However, the diktat has resulted in hardened hearts and intolerance, doing far greater evil.

Rise beyond not just idol worship but worship of any kind like worshipping sacred books and gurus. Let inner light become your guide, not religion or spiritual lure.

God

God stands for the inviolable metaphysical principles from where the universe and all its life has emerged. The principles are unknown.

The unknown cannot be touched by thought, named, and worshipped. We may enshrine our thoughts in temples, recite mantras and sing its praise. Thoughts cannot become God.

Nature can never be invoked or worshipped.

Worship

God represents the hidden principles of nature, and principles can neither bless nor curse.

Worship is a supplication with heavenly thought-feelings. They do not invoke god but influence by impinging similar vibrations upon others.

Prayers have consequences, not because of gods but because of their impact upon us and upon the subtle bodies of others in our surroundings.

Praying for blessings

People often pray to seek blessings.

Prayers for blessing is strangely an impurity. You may think them to be selfless and pure, but they are packets of self-oriented thought-feelings that crowd and pollute the subtle environment, and that is impurity.

Prayers only have consequences, and impurity begets impurity.

Guru

A guru is one who points out, like a directional signage.

Do we sit at the feet of a signage, sing its praise and worship it?

A guru is everywhere, in all things, if we open our eyes and see. Take the direction from what you observe and see and walk on. Only you are your best guru.

Siddhis

Siddhis are mystical powers.

They are manipulative selfish energies directed in the subtle media of thought-feelings. They act at an elemental level, unnaturally influencing the physical media to produce effects.

While people are enamoured with siddhis considering them godly, it is not easy to see how devastating their effect can be on karma.

Mantras

Mantras are packets of astral vibrations, powered by siddhis of its creator. They work by inducing a similar vibration in one's subtle body.

Mantras modify the psyche of those reciting them, albeit artificially, by magnifying similar properties in them.

Awareness of what the mantra is intended for, and consciously pouring in thought-energy can render mantras unusually powerful.

Spells

Spells are similar to mantras. While mantras work in subtle realms, spells work in grosser realms.

Mantras impact the psyche of the person reciting them. Spells impact those to whom the spells are directed.

Spells serve selfish and evil purposes. It is like throwing a stone at someone. Only those who are psychically vulnerable are affected by spells.

Guarding against spells

Practitioners of dark arts exploit the gullible with ritualistic charms, amulets, and counter-spells, making one even more vulnerable to spells.

The way of the White is to watch its effect fearlessly, thus building psychological immunity.

Being in close vicinity of someone who loves you dearly can be so very powerful, no spell can easily breach that fort.

Sin

Sin is a theological idea that instills fear. As theology influences society we are afraid of sin.

Acts have consequences. But fear results in guilt; not in a virtue called conscience.

Sin lives in minds of people, not just in perpetrators. The don'ts stir fear in everyone, doing far greater harm in the world.

Ancient languages

Sanskrit is a powerful ancient language, followed by Tamil and Telugu.

The far more powerful Senzar, now a lost language, had evolved over a million years and flourished in Atlantis.

Ancient languages are loaded with deep meaning. They create verbalisation that become barriers for evolution, as they tend to cage and channel thoughts along well-defined but archaic thought-patterns.

Tradition

Tradition belongs to the past. Culture, language, philosophies are all part of tradition.

Nature always draws down its curtain on tradition at end of every major race, guarding the past jealously, and forcing humanity to begin from scratch all over again.

Tradition can never bring revolution. This is known to very high intelligences who have guided evolution on earth.

Told and untold history

History is a doubled edged sword, carrying one away with rhetoric of historians.

There can be great learning from untold history covering gradual changes in civilization, contained in occult history. Told history covers shorter periods and recent events only, stirring sentiments and entertaining with their stories.

History speaks in whispers. What it loudly announces has only academic value.

Different kinds of energy

There are different kinds of energy, all descended from an all-pervading super-energy that has manifested as the worlds of nature.

Heat and light are its grossest state, and present in the physical environment.

Energies in the subtle environment are far more potent. Intelligence, when awakened as an outcome of spiritual evolution, can deal with different energies.

Aura

Every life, even plants and animals, have emanations called auras, visible to psychics.

The intelligent have a noticeable hallow. For a Buddha, his aura covers the entire valley.

Auras are subtle vibrations that impinge upon subtle bodies bringing them in harmony with theirs. Being in vicinity of enlightened beings can have remarkable though unseen effect.

Path to truth

There is the devotional path, ritualistic path, Tibetan path, Hindu path, Christian path, Islamic path and more, all claiming to lead to truth.

But truth is not static or fixed. There cannot be any fixed path to it.

Truth lies beyond time. It reveals itself when thoughts and efforts end, ending time. There is no path to it.

Will and will power

Will and will power are quite different things. They belong to very different levels of intelligence.

Will power is an outcome of strong personality, achieving objectives through unwavering emotional and intellectual determination.

Will is far beyond the reach of any determination or will power. It is a union with objectives, thus fulfilling itself instantly and effortlessly.

Spiritual experiences

Spiritual experiences are extremely rare, happening when the mind touches a subtlety beyond the reach of thought, thus ending duality.

They are incommunicable as the experiencer becomes the experience, and an experience can never narrate itself.

Don't be fooled by psychic experiences. They are not spiritual experiences. Spiritual experiences cannot be captured by thought and retained in memory.

Mystic

A mystic is one who knows because he can see but cannot express what he sees.

A mystic cannot verbalise his thoughts as he lives beyond the realm of articulable thoughts, in utter amazement.

Rare is a mystic who lives in awareness of his own amazement. He no longer remains a mystic. He goes beyond.

Kundalini

There are three energies from sun that together support life. Kundalini is one of them, enabling consciousness.

We have seven nerve centres called chakras through which kundalini flows inter-linking consciousness between our physical and subtle bodies.

Certain yogic exercises can activate the chakras in the subtle bodies for psychic abilities. Kundalini, when artificially aroused, can be dangerous.

Clairvoyance

Our environment is not just the physical world. There are several degrees of subtlety our five physical senses cannot sense.

Clairvoyance is a psychic ability to sense the subtle environment. There are several degrees of clairvoyance.

Clairvoyance is an outcome of bodily sensitivity when our spiritual nerve centres called chakras are activated.

Intelligence

Intelligence is a quality of perception and response. With intelligence one can live sensitively.

Intelligence is associated with our bodies. We have different kinds of bodies that express different kinds of intelligence.

Our intelligence is limited by the best our bodies can individually and collectively express.

Duality

Duality is an illusion of separateness when the mind imagines itself different from the whole. It is an outcome of self-protective thought that builds an image, a mirage, about itself.

Separateness creates an illusory distance. That distance is time. Time brings karma and suffering.

Awakening of intelligence ends the image, ending duality, time, and therefore suffering.

Gross and subtle

The gross is noticeable, the subtle is not. They are relative to each other.

The subtle has far greater powers. It influences the gross, never vice versa.

Our environment has different subtleties. One's intelligence can only sense and respond to the gross. A higher order of intelligence, which majorities do not have, is needed to sense the subtle.

Non-materialistic life

A materialistic life brings illusion and sorrow.

Materialism at its subtlest is present even in monks and sanyasis. While stoically abandoning worldly possessions they live in their thoughts for spiritual attainment.

A non-materialistic life is free from all possessions. Strangely, thought is our only possession, if one looks carefully, and materialistic too. Only thought needs sacrifice, not worldly life.

Different kinds of intelligence

Universal intelligence expresses itself as a spectrum of seven different subtleties of intelligence.

Grossest is physical intelligence, studied as nature's laws in physics. Emotional intelligence is subtler. Still subtler is intellect. But that is all we have.

Instant perception is a far subtler fourth kind of intelligence. It collapses time, ending duality. Can that be awakened?

Intuition

Intuition is commonly understood as stirring thoughts about a future event or outcome that occasionally or even often comes true. But that is not intuition.

Intuition is an outcome of clarity when thoughts have completely ceased. It is infallible unless corrupted by thought.

One cannot ask intuition for an answer. Intuition comes uninvited.

What is the "I"?

We think habitually and thinking results in thought.

Thought is a sediment of thinking. It has no present value as it belongs to the past. The sediments accumulate to become personality. That is the "I" in us.

The "I" is a calcified residue of thought that has become memory. It disappears when the mind cleans itself.

Discrimination

Discrimination is not just discriminating the right from the wrong, but also the more important from the less important.

It is often understood as an outcome of right thinking. But there is always an element of self in it, that corrupts.

Discrimination of a very different kind happens when one acts spontaneously from thought-free insight.

Desirelessness

Religions proscribe desirelessness. That is generally stoic, often lacking tenderness and compassion for one's own bodily tendencies.

Desire is an outcome of thought that revolves around the self, as if anchored to it. To be desireless is to be free from this anchor of thought.

Desirelessness comes gracefully on its own when one sees the bondage of thought.

Limits of the mind

The mind is limitless. It has potential for endless subtlety.

However, different kingdoms of life have their limits. A human mind is limited by thought. It can travel up till the subtlety to which thoughts can respond; nothing subtler.

Our mind can perhaps go beyond that limit when the hustle of thought is completely silent.

Adepts

Adepts are super-human entities with distinguishable existences as centres of energy but without any form or "I".

Awakening of a new kind of intelligence far subtler than intellect, has freed them from thought and memory, the "I"-creators and form-creators.

Adepts have evolved out of human life and are free from the cycle of death and rebirth.

World Teacher

A World Teacher comes in long intervals to plant seeds for a new awakening. The new being unknown is very difficult to see.

A World Teacher's teaching is for everyone, but only a few benefit. The majority must wait until ready.

Not every spiritual teacher is a World Teacher despite their popularity, or the label they may carry.

Enlightenment

Enlightenment is being a light unto oneself.

Enlightenment happens when one becomes unconditionally and irreversibly free from belief, knowledge or thought of any kind.

Enlightenment is not nirvana, moksha, union with God. They are ideas. Enlightenment is an outcome of meditation, which cannot be pursued. It comes into being upon awakening of intelligence.

How can I read minds?

Thought is matter, not energy. They are like material objects in the subtle realm of thoughts.

While we have consciousness in the subtle realms, we are not sensitive to them. Sensitivity called clairvoyance can be aroused artificially by awakening kundalini. Thoughts then become visible.

Reading thoughts is like peeping into someone's privacy. It is unbecoming for a noble person.

Dimensions of intelligence

There are dimensions of intelligence characterised by rising orders of subtlety.

The subtle remains hidden from intelligence grosser to it. The subtle can however comprehend all grosser kinds, influencing them; never vice versa.

Intellect, the thought-producer, developed to whatever extent can never awaken the next. It is a subtle dimension bringing instant perception. Only thought-free observation can trigger it.

Beauty is not skin deep

Beauty is not just in the face, but in one's inner beauty.

We radiate our thoughts and feelings. Prejudices show themselves as warts in our subtle body, making us ugly.

There is great charm when the subtle body is free from such warts or blemishes. That is what makes one glow in indescribable beauty.

Soul

Mind expresses itself as a centre, the "I".

It is an outcome of memory, becoming stronger, dominating, and self-protecting over time. That is the soul.

Soul is a bundle of self-oriented psychological memories. It creates an illusory division of 'self', resulting in time and karma. Awakening of intelligence dissolves the centre, freeing the mind from the illusion of soul.

Selfishness

Selfishness is an emotion of self-orientation with self-protecting and self-propagating tendencies.

Thought-feelings feed selfishness. Subtle thought-feelings result in stronger though hidden selfishness. As intellect drives thought-feelings, it results in a self.

One who sees selfishness in others is a very selfish person, as one finds others a threat. Selfishness ends when one rises beyond intellect ending the "me".

Selfishness has its use too

Selfishness is necessary for building our emotional and mental qualities. Without a strong centre, these qualities cannot be acquired.

Intellect awakens when emotional selfishness meets subtlety. After intellect is awakened, one begins to see its limitation. An urge then arises to go beyond limitations.

Selfishness has use as only then it can be abandoned to take one beyond.

Personal and impersonal

Anything self-oriented becomes a personal thing, creating division and therefore duality and karma. What is not, is impersonal.

Memories are strongly self-oriented. They are residues of thought-feelings and life experiences that one treasures as personal possessions.

Impersonal thoughts leave behind no residue and do not result in memory. They do not create duality, and therefore do not create karma.

Personality

Personality is a centre, the "I" in us. A strong personality implies a strong centre.

Personality tends to acquire and fiercely protect what it has acquired. It is steeped in physical, emotional, and intellectual capabilities but little else.

When adequately strengthened, personality begins to recognise its own futility. It then yearns to go beyond itself.

Karma

Karma is a law of cause-effect of our thoughts, feelings and actions.

They collectively impact our environment, whose effect is experienced by everyone, though differently. Effects become a new set of causes, and karma continues endlessly.

Karma is transcended when the mind becomes silent in the clarity of awareness.

Why evil prospers

Evil becomes heavy or gross over time. It strengthens the centre, the "I", but in a debased way as the evil always prosper in power.

Therein lies its danger as awakening of subtle intelligence is greatly hindered.

Evil begets evil, and therefore it always prospers. The downhill continues until one encounters a pit. Then the fall is terrible.

Desire

Desire is born when thought compares its content and concludes that the grass yonder is greener.

Desire then becomes yet another sediment of thought, weighing down the mind with its delectable smell. Smells become odours when pursued, as new desires always arise.

Desire is a tendency that can never be satiated. They become our sorrows.

Ambition

Ambition is a desire. It expresses dissatisfaction for reality, for what we actually are in present circumstances.

Ambitions are powered by emotions that often lack determination. They are wishful thinking, rarely backed by the energy of focused thought-power.

Ambition is a hunger that is never satiated. Our ambitions become our sorrows.

Theist and atheist

Thoughts create sediments of conclusions, that calcify into beliefs.

An atheist and a theist are two sides of the same coin of thought and belief. Agnostics are fence-sitters, awaiting to conclude.

Awareness is free from beliefs. One living in awareness is neither a theist nor an atheist, and unconcerned with deciding so neither an agnostic.

Feelings

We live in an environment of subtleties with bodies of different kinds.

Apart from the physical, there is the subtle, an environment that only responds to feelings.

Our desire body lives in that environment, generating feelings. They pollute the pristine environment, influencing our desire body and also the subtle bodies of others they meet.

Why emotions sway us

We are easily swayed by emotions.

We evolve spiritually over great races, explains occultism. Emotions being grosser, was first to be developed over a vast period of million years. Evolutionary focus on intellect is barely 75,000 years.

That is why emotions touch the majorities more readily. Intellect will surely influence many and much more readily, but in a distant future.

Euphoria

Euphoria is an emotional outburst of joy and ecstasy.

There is a strange energy in it that drives away every thought, prejudice and all negativity instantly, filling the mind with a sense of utter fulfilment.

While all this may taper off and end quickly, there is tremendous release of energy when euphoria is at its peak.

Thoughts

Beyond the subtlety of feelings is yet another environment far subtler, that only responds to thoughts.

We have a thought body that generates thought-packets whenever we think. Thoughts being tangible, pollute the thought environment.

We live a cauldron of polluted thought-feelings that impairs clarity unless the mind is very quiet and vibrantly alert to see beyond thought.

Vacuum of thoughts

While emotional outbursts can clear heaviness in a burst of emotional energy, it is just the opposite for thought.

New thoughts strike not during an outburst of thought, but only in vacuum of thought when the mind is completely relaxed.

Thinking forcibly only churns the old. Relaxing by music or games, lightens and rejuvenates the mind.

Violence

Violence is a fiery emotion that burns its path. One can feel its throbbing heat.

It begins as a well-intention spark ignited by parents for competing and winning in life. The spark grows to become a raging fire, devouring us and everything it meets.

Violence is an enemy of love. Shun that desire to be ahead in life and win.

Achievements

Achievements are worldly attainments. They are memories that die with us.

It is a never-ending thirst, as a higher peak always comes to sight. They are meaningless pursuits of sorrow, because achievements isolate, and isolation is sorrow.

The only achievement in life is an awakening of intelligence to recognise the futility of all worldly achievements.

Physical suffering

Physical suffering is unavoidable. Advise and philosophies carry little meaning.

Physical suffering is greatly multiplied when we think about it. Watching passively how thought causes pain, though difficult to watch, can act like a balm.

If we can look at our body as a separate entity that it actually is and empathise with it, pain takes a different form.

Cheerfulness

Cheerfulness is a happy emotion which thought can never justify or bring.

It creates an aura where heaviness and gloom cannot easily enter. One may be surprised to learn that cheerfulness modifies outcomes, smoothening difficult events and bringing pleasantries.

Cheerfulness begets cheerfulness, and you fill the space around you with favourable outcomes and happiness.

Friends and enemies

Circumstances create friends and enemies.

Our greatest enemy is often our best friend, only distanced by circumstances and selfishness. Worldly memories end quickly after we die, ending worldly circumstances, relations, and all enemies.

Similarity of temperament, tendencies and affinities bring enemies together as friends after death. Do we have to wait until we die?

Mystery in life science

The reason why life exists has remained a big mystery in life science.

There are three very different and non-interconvertible kinds of energy from sun, *fohat*, *kundalini* and *prana*, that together are responsible for all life. *Prana* energy integrates life at a micro-biological level.

Discovering and studying *prana* is needed for break-through discoveries in life sciences.

The inanimate have life

The inanimate have life. They are living entities!

There are various kingdoms of evolving life, and the inanimate is one of them. It is primitive life-form preceding the vegetable kingdom.

They have group-souls, not individual souls with intelligence that respond only to physical forces. They evolve over incalculable periods to finally become life-essence of the vegetable kingdom.

Life after death

When we die, our physical body dies cutting us sharply from the physical world.

Our desire and thought bodies however remain intact and we live in full consciousness in the subtle worlds of feelings and thought.

Afterlife is far more pleasant in absence of physical suffering. We make new friends and live our feelings and thoughts.

Near-death experience

Sometimes the mind thinks it has died. This induces consciousness to slip through a narrow silvery etheric cord connecting the physical and subtle bodies.

This being thought-driven is captured by the brain as a near-death-experience.

Actual death can never be experienced as the etheric cord snaps, instantly cutting off the brain. Near-death-experiences are only hallucinations about dying.

Past life memories

Past life contents cannot exist, as death ends them all.

Death is like taking a vessel, melting it down and recasting a new vessel. However, the quality, that is, tendencies that characterise our life, find continuity as the material of the new vessel.

Only quality is a carry-over. But the vessel casted is new, with no past, no memory.

Past life divination is unreliable

Every event is stored in an indelible memory of nature called akasha in the subtle realm of the mental world.

Most diviners can only access the less subtle astral realm where akashic records also appear but as unreliable spasmodic shadows.

Divination covering past lives become particularly error-prone as personalities also change making it near-impossible to track them reliably.

Hell, Narka, and Jahannam

Hell, Narka, and Jahannam are frightening theological beliefs about afterlife, stirring fear in gullible minds.

We all suffer our emotional tendencies while living. These tendencies linger on after we die but can never get worse.

We suffer this residue in immediate afterlife. Fear instilled by religion only make it worse, causing desperation and panic.

Heaven, Swarga, and Jannah

Heaven, Swarga, and Jannah are alluring theological beliefs.

There are different phases in afterlife, and the heaven-world is a phase after emotional energies have dissipated. We then live our imagination free from fear, as happy daydreams.

This happiness is for everyone, depending on intensity of one's thinking tendencies. Even the worst criminal has his share of heavenly happiness.

Is death painful to be feared?

Sacred books say that death is painful. Is that so?

The etheric cord at the navel snaps at death, instantly cutting off the body and brain from the mind, to relate any pain. Moreover, our five senses cannot sense the dying event as the brain is cut off.

Events leading to death may be painful, but death is certainly painless.

What happens after we die

Our physical body dies cutting us from the physical world.

We continue to live in our desire body where our emotional tendencies bring suffering. This dies too in a 'second death'. Freed from emotions we then live our thoughts happily in our thought-body.

Even that happiness ends. Seeds of mental tendencies remain, later sprouting into a new life.

Addiction after death

Addiction is a terrible habit resulting in bodily urges.

We lose our physical bodies at death. Emotional tendencies now dominate, resulting in psychological urges. This makes one terribly restless as the dead person cannot identify the cause. The suffering is without respite, seeming unending as sense of time is lost.

Kick those habits before you die.

Death and rebirth

Death is a complete ending of memory, a residue that must be emptied.

Intelligence is a quality and not a content or residue like memory. It never dies.

Only body with all its content is lost forever at death. It can never reincarnate. Intelligence, now enriched with life-experiences, finds continuity as a new life.

Mourning the dead

"My son died very young," she said, "I cannot wipe away my tears."

Memories cannot bring back the dead. The dead only respond to feelings. Your tears can only bring agony.

Happy memories will also bring him sorrow. They get worse whenever kindled, making the dead earth-bound. He can never come back to life. Nostalgia is a suffering.

Immortality

Death is an ending of our body, thoughts, and memories. We fear death because we treasure memories, associating ourselves with it.

Can we live in thought-free awareness, meeting the present directly with intelligence not through memories or thought?

Then nothing will accumulate in our mind, and there will be nothing to die. Therein lies immortality.

Suicide

Suicide is a despicable act, a great betrayal.

Our body has an independent life, put under our care. We have no right to end it. It is murder.

Suicides are outcomes of suicidal tendencies. When tendencies have driven one to the edge, just a nudge can trigger the dastardly act. One cannot blame another for abetting suicide.

Beyond Knowledge

Knowledge is merely brilliance in organization of ideas and not wisdom. The truly wise person goes beyond knowledge.

Confucius

BEYOND KNOWLEDGE

Knowledge belongs to the past, discovered by scientists and sages. It is concrete, material and stale. When we use any old object, there is the stale and impurity in it. That can never lead us to the new, to what is not contained.

One needs to discard knowledge of every kind to discover what lies beyond. Therein lies the secret of inward flowering.

Thought upon recognising the limitation of knowledge seeks to go beyond it. A bud then appears waiting to blossom.

Thinking

Thinking produces thought and thought the thinker. It produces a centre, the "I".

Thinking cannot operate without a centre. It may stretch itself but never become free. Thinking wears away the brain, draining away energy.

Observation and awareness take over when thinking ceases, bringing clarity. We can effortlessly live in the present with clarity without expending energy.

Thought is limited

Thought needs a fulcrum to operate, a reference. Thinking is entirely relational, as if anchored to the reference.

The reference is always memory of some knowledge or belief. The mind cannot free itself while riding a wagon of memories. It limits the mind.

To go far and beyond, the mind must step down from the wagon.

Illusion

Illusion is what we think it is, while it is not.

Whatever we think and believe to be true may be an illusion, as there is always the deeper hidden from us.

Illusion is born from thought. Illusions end when the thinker ends. Then it is observation and there is no illusion about it.

Delusions

A delusion is a false belief or opinion.

Every belief depends upon some knowledge it is based. Knowledge is essentially psychological in nature, as new discoveries have always overhauled the old since ages.

Any knowledge or belief is a delusion from a different perspective or depth. One needs to learn, not to crack delusions, but to go beyond them.

Ending of illusion

Thought-free observation brings awareness. There is always a separation between the observer, the "you" and the observed, else observation cannot happen.

Observation shows the observer it is its memories that has been observing all along. This ends the illusory separation, ending the illusion of observation.

What remains behind is awareness of a much deeper kind.

Do we have a past

We build an image from an image-free state at birth, giving it continuity until we die. This becomes our identity, the 'me'.

Time begins when continuity begins, ending when continuity ends. Past exists, but only within the band of continuity.

The 'me' has no past before the image was created. We have no past.

Predestination and freewill

Predestination and free will are two sides of the same coin of belief.

Free will cannot exist as there is no choice in cause-effect causation. Predestination cannot also exist in the timelessness and pathlessness of energy.

When self is an image and nonexistent, whom will predestination or free-will be applicable for? They are only abstract ideas.

Does free will exist?

Free will is an action born from a choice that is not tethered to the past and is complete free.

But every action is necessarily conditioned as they are outcomes of a chain of causation of many factors from the past.

As an unconditioned or free choice cannot exist, free will cannot exist. It is only deception.

Predestination is an idea

If free-will does not exist, does it not imply predestination?

Energy is unaffected by time, knowing only the present, neither the past nor future. It is living, dynamic, ever-changing, in a pathless path. It has no fixed or pre-existing destiny.

Predestination is a myth created by limitation of thought that cannot comprehend pathlessness.

We evolve by building images

There is only energy, flowing in patterns. Repeated patterns result in matter.

The mind builds images by lending permanency to these patterns that have become matter, causing an illusory stagnation of energy.

The mind eventually recognises images as transitory and false but continues to build newer and subtler ones, as life climbs a ladder of subtle images to evolve.

Images bring sorrow

We build images about ourselves and spend our lives protecting them, strengthening false identities.

The image is not a fact. We are nobodies. The flowing river of life is not a cesspool of stagnant water.

Recognising this fact ends struggles and sorrows. We unite with the river whose waters flow unhindered past all hurdles of life.

Cause of suffering

Life embodies suffering. We suffer physical pain. That is unavoidable. But our real suffering, sorrow, is far more devastating.

Sorrow is an outcome of our psychological memories. Our likes, dislikes, attachment, hatred, jealousy, ambitions, everything has its origin in memories.

Memories end by dying to every passing moment. There is constant renewal in the brain and suffering ends.

Sorrow

Memory is the root cause of sorrow.

Sorrow comes into being when thought brings memories to the present for the mind to live in a house of nostalgia and tears.

Sorrow ends when there is complete attention to the present. This results in ending time, therefore ending memories and sorrow.

Presence of mind

Presence of mind comes into being when one lives entirely in the present, neither in the past nor in the future.

Life is a kaleidoscope of aromas and colours. But thought tries to verbalise them from memories, calling them experiences and building a castle to live.

Watching thoughts brings the presence of mind.

Logical mind

A logical mind arranges its content skillfully to discover hidden patterns.

A logical mind brings about better understanding but only for old content, filling the mind with new patterns of the old. It never replaces or removes the old, even though we think.

A logical mind in spite of all its intellectual ability, is inherently mechanical, imitative, and rarely perceptive.

Continuity

The mind habitually seeks continuity.

It is entirely psychological, as it is continuity of beliefs, memories, knowledge and thoughts. That is why they accumulate, becoming a centre called self. Time, fear and suffering are its outcome. What if continuity ends?

Death ends continuity. But, do we have to wait until we die?

Ending continuity

Thinking is so very habitual that it needs extraordinary effort to end continuity.

Can we just watch our thoughts with great attention effortlessly, and live as we normally do? There would be no time or space for new gathering when we are completely attentive. Continuity will find its own break in the passion of watchfulness.

Psychological effortlessness ends continuity.

Memories

Memories, both physical and psychological, are contents gathered from life-experiences.

Physical memory is needed for practical life, but psychological memory becomes a burden. It is a residue in the content with no useful purpose.

Our body is a container for memories. Death ends the container with all its content.

Conscious and subconscious mind

There is our conscious mind that has been educated and groomed from childhood.

There is also the subconscious, a mind that has lived through all experiences of humanity that drives the conscious mind.

When we watch the conscious mind, the subconscious reveals itself and transforms. It unifies with the conscious ending divisions and becoming a whole.

Subconscious mind

The mind has its content of memories, but not in compartments called conscious and subconscious.

Memories not on the surface are classified by psychologists as subconscious mind.

Conscious or subconscious, memories belong to the past. They only burden the mind. What created them is immaterial. When emptied, the conscious and subconscious lose their distinction to become unified as one.

Death

Life means consciousness. It is an outcome of intelligence, a quality of the mind that evolves with life experiences.

But we gather memories as well, burdening the mind with content. Intelligence can become free to flower when the contents are emptied.

Death comes as a benediction, emptying the mind of all its content.

Meditation

Meditation is becoming aware without choice and without judging what we observe, and therefore without losing energy.

Purposeful meditation is not meditation as that tells us what to do. It drains energy and steals freedom.

Meditation is living in effortless awareness with equal attention towards everything. It is the greatest art of living.

Meditation and emptiness

Meditation empties the mind, but that does not result in emptiness. The contents rush back when efforts are withdrawn.

Emptiness comes into being naturally when nothing is gathered. It comes into being when the mind can meet the present directly and not through the support of memory and thought.

Emptiness is the highest state of meditation.

Why should we meditate?

Meditation keeps the mind empty by not living with thoughts that always gather content, but by living with intelligence.

Various methods are advocated, but they all kill meditation rather than enable it as methods are thought-driven.

Why meditate, is a wrong question. Meditation happens naturally like breathing when we are aware, unless interfered by thought with intentions to meditate.

Mental strength

Mental strength is an outcome of mental energy.

We constantly dissipate this energy by thinking. Thinking is a struggle between pairs of opposites like this or that, right or wrong. It causes friction, draining energy, and mental strength is lost.

Ending of thought ends this friction and dissipation. It brings enormous mental strength to power spontaneous living.

Thought is material

Thinking is a conflict between what is and what the mind wants it to be. Thought, its residue, is matter, not energy.

A thinking mind is a material mind, a mind made dull by the repeated pattern of thinking that drains energy.

Tremendous energy can be released when the mind breaks every pattern, ending thought and matter.

Dull mind

A dull mind follows and lives with the known. It learns from books, gurus, and everlastingly imitating. It cannot think for itself.

Sitting in postures doing breathing exercises, reciting mantras, practicing yoga and austerities, also makes the mind dull in its act of repetition.

A dull mind is dried and hardened. It can never discover the beauty of the unknown.

Thinking makes the mind dull

Many of us believe that thinking keeps the mind healthy and sharp. The truth is different.

Thinking causes inward friction, draining energy. It is a repetitive process, tiring the brain and making it dull.

The brain recovers its sharpness and is rejuvenated in the stillness between two thoughts, as in the silence the mind meets universal energy.

Answers make the mind dull

We ask questions because we do not know the art of keeping questions alive in our minds and watching them passionately.

If we do that, questions begin to whisper their answers bringing learning and wisdom, not knowledge.

Answers when fed makes the mind dull and obese with vain knowledge. Asking questions, like drugs, is addiction with a similar effect.

Deja vu

There are rare occasions when we encounter something and are surprised to have known it before.

Has the present existed before and already lived by us, and therefore remembered?

When the mind is unknowingly silent, it recognises that the past had contained the present. That familiarity brought forward from the past is deja vu.

Logic

Logic is an instrument for thinking.

It needs a point of reference to operate, some assumption or past memory. It can build around the reference wonderfully, yet it is always tethered to the reference.

Logic can never free itself from the reference, often getting stuck in invisible self-justifying loops thereby limiting usefulness of thought.

Thinking by elimination

We generally think by logically constructing possibilities to come to a conclusion.

A different way is by eliminating what is not or cannot be. Flashes of remarkable outcome strike a mind when it is only concerned with elimination.

It is the highest form of thinking as it breaks preset mental patterns. There is far greater surety in it.

Experiences

We think experiences are all-important in life. That is only an illusion.

Experiences turn into memories that remain to haunt us in future.

Experiences belong to the past. They have no real value as they do not change the quality of mind in any way. They only make the mind slothful and dull with new biases.

Experiencing

Experiencing lives in the present. It is not a content, like experience, which is just its illusory sediment.

Experiencing can never be recognised by thought as time collapses in the instantaneous present.

Silently and subtly, experiencing modifies the quality of the mind when we are alert and watchful. There is enormous value in experiencing, not in experience.

The brain and mind

The brain contains all experiences, knowledge and memories. It is always conditioned.

But love and compassion, being qualities, are beyond conditioning.

The mind is limitless but finds expression only through the brain. The brain has limitations, but we further limit it by living in images in fixed patterns of thought, and not in the freedom of awareness.

Experiencing oblivion

Can we experience oblivion? Only an experiencer who has isolated oneself from the whole, experiences anything.

So, experiences are only illusory projections of the mind as the whole is undivided.

Oblivion can come when the self ends. There is no experiencer, experience, or realisation in oblivion. There is only existence, and existence cannot know itself. Oblivion cannot be 'experienced'.

Pride in our past

Some people are proud of the past, their country, religion, great rishis and scientists, and their rich heritage.

The past is dead and history. It is a garland of stale flowers that only make us poor.

What matters is the present, what we are now. Fresh flowers can never blossom in the soil of the past.

Authorities

Authority is an expert, guru, or even a holy book that you believe can illuminate your path.

But truth is never fixed; it has no path. Authority is only a false image created by you, that soon becomes a bondage.

The journey is pathless. Only freedom from all kinds of authorities can become our light.

Pride in knowledge

Life entices us with savoury jars of knowledge. But once inside there is an obsession for more.

Knowledge results in obesity of "I know". The one who says so knows not that he does not know.

Intelligence lies in living frugally in the awareness of "I do not know". Knowledge makes the mind obese, lethargic and proud.

Tolerance

Tolerance is an acceptance of reality, not self-imposed by thought.

Our thoughts make us intolerant when expectations are not met. But a child cannot become an adult overnight.

Tolerance is an outcome of awareness. It is a fruit of insight. We cannot learn or practice to become more tolerant. Only insight results in tolerance.

Determination

Determination is a tremendous focus of the mind, aligning and directing all its thought energy in one direction.

Thought has unbridled power, and determination can produce unimaginable worldly results.

Determination however impedes spiritual flowering. It acts like an anchor, pegging the mind to its thought centre, the ego, and not releasing it.

Temperaments have beauty

Temperament is a tendency, a quality of our bodies, not content.

Emotional and thinking tendencies are qualities of our emotional and mental bodies, our two distinctly different subtle bodies. These bodies influence our emotions and thoughts.

Temperament, good, bad or even fearsome, can have great beauty. They glow in their natural colours when free from memories and prejudices.

Habits

Habit is a mechanical behaviour. They become our natural tendencies we find hard to resist or change.

We try to consciously change habits by effort and will. This however feeds them with energy, making the groove of habits deeper.

Habits change not when they are denied or suppressed, but when accepted and watched very intently.

Foolishness

Foolishness is an unintelligent act. As actions follow thought, foolishness is an outcome of unintelligent thinking.

Thought is always limited, so unintelligent. It is easy to criticise or laugh at someone, but the other person can see foolishness in us too.

Spontaneous action born from clarity is free from thought, and so cannot be foolish.

Hypocrisy

Hypocrisy is a pretence of higher standards or nobler beliefs. Pretence is a despicable act and hypocrites are liars.

Sometimes we point out the miserable acts of others, often criticising them. Hypocrisy is hidden in criticism because if the act was alien to us, there would only be tender empathy, never criticism.

Hypocrites make a society sick.

Decrying sordid acts

Sordid acts make us shudder. We decry them, longing for justice and punishment.

Can we observe the sharp surge of disgust and anger in us? That indicates presence of the same evil in us too, as else there will only be compassion.

Feel gently for others. Our anger only nourishes the evil thought-feeling, and the malady spreads.

Fear

Fear is always about something. It is always at a distance, in future, separated by time. It ends when the distance ends.

While fear is real, what we are afraid of is an idea, and ideas are born from thought.

Thoughts cannot arise when there is complete attention. Attention lives in the present, with freedom from fear.

Root of all fear

The mind lives in memories. Memories are only beliefs.

Every action, if observed carefully, is based on beliefs. It is a pattern the mind has become terribly accustomed to, dependent and addicted.

That addiction is the root of all fear. The mind fears emptiness. It does not know what will happen if beliefs suddenly go away.

Lust

Lust comes into being when pleasure becomes a driver for an image created by thought.

It is a desire driven by thought-feelings, that keep growing and gathering until it explodes in a climax of fulfilment. But, then what?

The delight in lust is gone immediately after its fulfilment, leaving one very shallow and hollow.

Passion

Passion is yet another quality of the mind. It is a presence, not content but quality, unrelated to either feeling or thinking.

Passion has no driver, no motive. Unlike lust, it does not seek fulfilment. Yet it pervades the mind and one's whole being, becoming a driver for anything.

Awareness breeds passion. Love is an outcome of passion in awareness.

Sex

Sex is often looked upon as taboo and proscribed in religions and by gurus. It corrupts when it becomes a pursuit of sensation.

Sex born from love is entirely different. There is complete abandonment of problems, and no lust or self in the act.

Denying sex is brutality, like cutting off one's ears and eyes.

Jealousy

Jealousy is an emotional vibration of a particular kind. It creates itchy-burning-restlessness in minds susceptible to it, bringing psychological suffering.

Jealousy brings restlessness when triggered by comparing thoughts.

Living with the feeling, accepting it as that is our actual nature, and intently watching how thought easily plays upon this emotion to bring suffering, can end jealousy.

Distraction

Distraction means wavering from a path. It demands focus. We expend energy.

Where there is self, there is a path for attainment. Attainment can only make the illusion called self a bigger illusion, a glorious mirage.

Attention, which comes about when there is no self, only anonymity, ends distraction by ending interest in attainments.

Disenchantment in life

"Nothing excites me anymore in life," he said.

When the mind seeks gratification from the senses and pursues excitement, the soil dries up quickly and the plant dries.

Tenderness comes only when one ends his search for sensory excitement and instead watches life intently with tremendous attention. Do it now, not tomorrow, before you turn into deadwood.

How to live without desire

Thought creates an object at a distance and that distance is time. Time gives birth to desire.

One cannot reach it. Ending of desire happens when thoughts become silent and distances collapse.

Desire to live without desire is a desire too. It is a wish to become what one is not. Accepting desire ends desire.

Insight

Insight is born from clarity. Like clarity, insight cannot be gathered and shared. Insights do not burden the mind like knowledge.

Clarity is an outcome of observation. It comes into being when the buzz of thought is completely silent.

Insight lives beyond the field of time. It is deathless, getting deeper and clearer with growing clarity.

Spiritual life

"How can I live a spiritual life?" he asked.

There are only three things. First, observe and remain aware. Second, do not waste your energy by carrying beliefs and thoughts. Third, accept yourself and your circumstances, graciously and gratefully.

When imbued and lived, just these three things can remarkably transform your consciousness.

Pity and compassion

Pity is an emotion that arises in a sensitive mind. We wish we could do something about it.

Pity arises when we separate ourselves from the suffering.

A different action takes place when we look at it directly. It ends the gap between us and the sufferer, resulting in compassion. It is the highest action.

Illusion of learning

Learning from study, knowledge or even from experiences is impermanent and illusory. Only content is gathered but wiped off completely at death.

The mind learns in the stealth of thought-free awareness. It cannot know it has learnt as thought cannot capture it.

Only such learning is permanent, modifying the quality of the mind and resulting in spiritual evolution.

Knowledge and wisdom

Knowledge is the known, captured by thought and expressed in words. It is a content of the mind, gathered from experience, and can be shared.

Wisdom is an outcome of intelligence. Like intelligence, it is a quality of the mind, not content. It illuminates, bringing clarity.

Wisdom cannot be gathered. It is personal and cannot be shared.

Listening in denial

Right listening is so complete that one can hear beats of the false together with whispers of truth.

It is neither accepting, discarding, or judging anything. It is listening with our heart without building images yet looking with passive denial, that is, negatively.

Listening with passive denial is the highest form of listening.

Seeing is action

Every action is preceded by thought. So says the *Dhammapada* too.

Thought is always limited. Actions born from thought must also be limited. They create disturbances. Nature recoils to restore harmony.

Seeing, born from thought-free awareness, brings compassion. It is the highest action. It does not disturb but unites with cosmic energy. Seeing is action!

Truth and falsehood

Should we side with the truth even if truth entails suffering?

Truth looks at false and calls it false. False looks at truth and says how it is also false. They are inseparable. What then is right action?

An intelligent mind has no choice. It sees the false in truth and the truth in false. That very seeing results in the right action.

Good and evil

Wherever there is the good, there is evil. The two are inseparable.

The good is a tendency to rise into subtle, from matter to energy. Evil is a force preventing change, dragging the mind into gross and matter.

Evil dies a natural death when we live with the good without fueling evil by not fighting it.

Verbalising eludes learning

The brain relates whatever we see to what we know, giving it a name. That is verbalising.

We do not see the river but an image called river, seen through a lens of the past. A newborn learns because it does not verbalise.

Verbalising ends by dying to our memories. The new is revealed, bringing a new birth and learning.

Living without struggle

Sometimes we come to the crossroads of right and wrong. A struggle with our conscience then begins. We lose energy.

Can we live without the struggle, doing whatever comes naturally to us and unconcerned with values and morality?

The energy conserved begins to feed awareness. Awareness may not change our actions but can cure tendencies.

Identity breeds violence

We all want peace. History is evidence that we seek it through violence.

We live with identities and want the identity to live in harmony with other identities. But identity means separation, and separation brings conflict. Identity breeds violence.

We can never have peace until we have discarded every identity, we have created for ourselves.

Violence and nonviolence

Violence and nonviolence are a pair of inseparable ideas created by a centre that has separated itself from reality to take a self-protecting side.

A transformation happens when the mind sees that separation or division is at the root of all violence.

That ends the separation and the centre, transcending both violence and nonviolence.

Purpose of life

Does life really have a purpose? We can invent ideas like enlightenment, union with God and so on. But ideas can never become purpose.

To discover one must live life first. But we have never done that. It is our thoughts and beliefs that have lived their lives.

If life has any purpose, it is to live.

Philosophy can harden hearts

Philosophy belongs to the subtle realms of thought.

Some of us are inclined towards philosophising, even misfortunes of others. Isn't that cold and unfeeling?

Philosophy is a doubled edged sword. It can harden hearts with philosophical justification, distancing one from compassion. Never allow philosophy to completely grip your mind. Allow the mind to flower in the tenderness of compassionate feelings.

Achievement in life

Becoming somebody with enormous success, influence and respect, is a great challenge in life. Not only our effort but some luck is also needed.

However, a nobody has far greater value. Immensity seeks out only empty vessels.

Becoming empty is the greatest achievement in life. It needs no struggle to become. Not even luck.

Time and space

Time is a measure from beginning to end. It is distance or space. Time is space.

Time and space are only relative to the observer, therefore illusions.

Illusions end when the observer recognises it is not different from what it is observing. This ends the separation between the observer and the observed. Time and space collapse and end.

Why we do not change

We wish to change but find it difficult.

If we observe, we will see we have created an image for ourselves, and all our efforts are concerned with bringing a change in that image. That cannot change us.

A fundamental change can happen when we see this fact. The very seeing brings about a dramatic change.

Energy and matter

There are only two things, energy and matter. They are inseparable, interdependent, and inter-convertible.

Energy operating in any pattern results in a residue, which is matter. It may not be physical matter but simply matter, not energy.

Energy is all-pervading and infinite, whereas matter exists as lumps or forms. It lacks dynamism, impedes energy and results in time.

Instant perception

Thinking is a movement in time through logical deduction and conclusion, which the mind gathers as memory.

Instant perception sees it all in a glance. It is free from thought and therefore free from conclusion and time. Nothing is gathered and the mind remains empty.

Instant perception needs extraordinary intelligence. Rather, it is intelligence of a very high order.

Instinctual intelligence

Thought links the past to the present bringing continuity and memory. We are so very dependent we cannot live without memories and thoughts.

Instinct, which is instinctual intelligence, begins to work when continuity ends. This is different from memory and intellect.

We can end memories and live practical lives in thought-free awareness with instinctual intelligence as our guide.

Love communicates

Spoken and written words and our deeds communicate. But there is distortion.

The recipient is often preoccupied with thoughts, biases, interpretations. So is the communicator. Is there any way?

It is in the empathy of silence. Not even a word is needed. Empathy enters the mind unawares and in stealth. There is love. Love communicates.

Empathy

When we see suffering, we feel miserable about it. We hope we could do something for it. That is pity, not empathy.

We think we must soothe the wounds, but that is sympathy.

When we see the totality, there is accompaniment of our heart and mind with the sufferer. That is empathy. It is an outcome of love.

The future is now

We are forever concerned about the future, wanting it better, safer, kinder.

Whatever we imagine is a projection of our experiences of a past which we have never lived fully.

If we live fully and intelligently in the present, accepting what we are in reality, the future is not a distant dream. It lives in the 'now'.

The real sanyasi

There is a great sense of simplicity and humility when one recognises oneself as a nobody.

Knowledge becomes purposeless and immaterial. There is no one to possess it. Thinking ends, for there is no one to think for.

One joins the river of life, living without any pretence or urge. That is a real sanyasi.

Beyond Thought

The mind, with its incessant weaving of patterns, is the maker of time; and with time there is fear, hope and death.

Jiddu Krishnamurti

BEYOND THOUGHT

Thought can discover, which then becomes new-found knowledge. We can feed upon knowledge, imitating what it contains, but remain imprisoned within its fixed pattern in the kingdom of the known.

The kingdom of the unknown lies beyond patterns of thought. One has to be spotlessly clean and not dirtied by knowledge and memories to enter into it.

Dismount from your horse of thoughts and feelings and walk barefoot with love and compassion as your guide. Only then the gates of the kingdom of unknown may open and allow you to pass.

Fresh air is needed for flowering. Open those windows of the mind to drive out the stench of the stale and stagnated, and allow fresh air to come in.

Discovery

Curiosity of observation is extinguished as our mind falls into a habitual groove of thinking and concluding. It is this pattern that prevents discovery.

The brain always verbalises observation to conclude from contents gathered in past. The innocence to discover the new is lost.

Thought-free watchfulness breaks this pattern. And there is discovery.

Observation

Observation is watchfulness through the eyes of intelligence without the burden of beliefs, knowledge or thought.

When we recognise what we observe, it is an earlier thought about it, never the now.

Observation is discovery. It is always new and nameless. Observation begins when the thinker and his thought ends.

Observation brings order

Observation is freedom from logic. It brings clarity. There is beauty because it reveals the order and harmony of nature.

The order contains remarkable logic, but of a kind that can never be verbalised or explained.

Observation lives in the present. What we think we have observed is not observation, but chaos created by thought.

Awareness

Awareness is wakefulness. It is a natural flower of intelligence.

Awareness is not an outcome of thought or effort. These narrow our focus into concentration and exclusion, tainting and killing awareness.

The flower of awareness blossoms when the mind is free from thoughts and feelings, yet alert and watchful.

Awareness in sleep

"Can I have awareness when asleep?" he asked.

Awareness is our natural state when thoughts have ceased. We can never know when aware.

Awareness comes in stealth when the mind is silent. It continues uninterrupted in sleep, or even under anaesthesia. Awareness is also there after we die.

Attention

Attention is not an outcome of effort. Efforts drain energy, whereas attention brings energy.

Attention is not focus. Focus excludes what the mind is not interested in.

Attention comes naturally when the 'me' is pushed aside bringing anonymity. The mind becomes directionless but sees everything effortlessly, without losing energy. Anonymity breeds attention.

Understanding and clarity

Normally we seek understanding, followed by acceptance.

Understanding is a great illusion. It is a dissection of contents in mind, our memories and beliefs, but little else.

Clarity comes when the mind discovering how meaningless understanding is, rejects it entirely and looks directly. There is neither acceptance nor rejection in clarity. The mind simply sees.

The trap called thinking

Thinking is our highest faculty. But there are still higher faculties like instant perception.

To awaken the subtle, the mind must rise above thought. Thinking is a trap as it involves effort.

The mind can rise to the subtle only when vibrantly alert but without effort for any attainment. That ends thought. Only effortlessness can deliver.

Ancient wisdom

Ancient wisdom contains gems of thought, philosophies, and truth. What is their real worth?

Their study and pursuit only feed intellect. That may enrich us, but we need to go beyond to awaken intelligence.

To go beyond, one must travel naked in thought-free awareness. The journey has no path, no direction, no book, no study.

Energy can answer questions

Every urge produces energy, but the energy quickly dissipates in conflict when pursued.

A question is an urge too, producing energy depending on the intensity and urgency of the question.

This energy is preserved when there is a complete denial of pursuit to seek out answers. It presents answers on a silver platter when seeking has completely ended.

Thinking and instant perception

We think to conclude and comprehend. Thinking expends energy, and involves time. The conclusion becomes a new content, burdening the mind.

Instant perception is seeing directly, instantly, and effortlessly. Energy is preserved, and the mind remains free without conclusions.

Instant perception brings clarity. It is aroused when the mind completely rejects thinking and only sees.

Difficulty in instant perception

Instant perception is difficult. It is sight, and one can never see through a haze of memories and thoughts.

Efforts cannot clear the haze, as effort implies thought that creates haze.

When thoughts are watched with inward silence, there is no nourishment. The haze thins out and fades. The sight becomes visible, bringing instant perception.

Logic and its ending

The brain works through logic. Logic is necessary to understand any problem of life.

However, to understand problems and resolve them completely, the brain must be completely free, even free from logic.

When the mind sees this fact logically, the very seeing frees the mind, bringing logic-free clarity and awareness. Logic is needed to transcend itself.

Matter creates time

Energy moving in a pattern is matter. Thinking, which always operates in a fixed pattern results in thought-forms, which is matter too.

Thought, and even every other kind of matter, has a beginning and ending and continuity in between. Matter ends when its energy ends.

Time is an outcome of matter. Matter creates the continuity called time.

Evolution

The past, present and the future is entirely contained as a property of matter upon manifestation. The acorn contains the oak.

How evolution will happen exists logically all along, in minute details, but revealed over its lifespan.

We call it evolution as we live in the domain of time and cannot see across the entire spectrum of time.

Manifestation

Manifestation is coming into being. It is Creation, existence. What manifests is matter, manifesting from energy.

Time begins with manifestation and ends upon obscuration, annihilation, or pralaya.

Existence has no cause, for it has no past. What exists, exists. We cannot question it. We cannot invent a cause. We can only accept it with utter humility.

There is no choice in freedom

Freedom is unconditional, even from the slave-master who says, "You have every freedom you want".

We want freedom for future outcomes. But outcomes lie in a nonexistent future, created by the bondage of our knowledge and memories. Every choice is bondage in disguise.

Freedom comes when we become free from choice. There is no choice in freedom, only awareness.

Knowledge, humility, and learning

Sacred books like the Gita, Upanishads, Vedas, Vedanta, Scriptures bring only bookish knowledge, never learning. They create vain pundits.

When one sees how knowledge is vanity as all pundits end at death, one discards all sacred books taking *sanyas* from knowledge to watch life in the humility of a nobody.

Learning that now comes unawares, lives beyond death.

Liberation

Liberation means liberation from one's self, the "I" principle in us.

It is a liberation from the bondage of thought, and therefore liberation from karma or cause-effect and also from matter, time and space.

Liberation happens when one's intelligence awakes in a new dimension that lies beyond intellect and thought. This ends the cycle of death and rebirth too.

Ending of time

Time is a property of matter, a measure of unbroken distance between its creation and ending. Time ends when continuity breaks.

Time brings suffering, which can only end when time ends.

Thought being material, brings time. Suffering can end by ending psychological association with thought. Dying to every passing moment breaks continuity of thought, thus ending time.

Beauty

Nature is abound with beauty.

There is beauty in the skies and mountains, in the rivers and living beings. There is beauty in the storm that devastates, in the fire that rages and devours.

There is harmony without prejudice as nature mirrors the truth of life until vandalised by thought. Truth untouched by thought is beauty.

There is only the present

Is there really a past? The past has never existed. It is always the present. Even the future does not exist.

History means past but is entirely contained in the present. So are thoughts and beliefs. They belong to the present but create illusions of past and future.

The eternal present becomes visible when one recognises the illusion of thought.

Do what you love

Holy books, temples and gods, are weeds of pretense and we worship them in vain.

When we do what we love to do, we learn. That learning becomes wisdom.

Then wisdom becomes our temple, actions our prayers, and people our gods. We can blossom in such a garden without pretense when we do what we love.

Real success is love

Success is a lonely road, distancing you from life, to crown you a king. Nothing can be sadder.

One must learn to descend from the high peak and take everyone along. A different heart is needed.

Success is in togetherness. One must become a pathway for everyone, not the king. Then there is real success. It is love.

Love cannot be practised

Many great teachers have talked about love.

Love cannot be learnt and practised. It comes into being when the mind becomes aware and extraordinarily sensitive. It is an outcome when the mind has ended all images, ending the illusion of separateness.

Love is our natural state of being in the compassion of image-free awareness.

Love

Love is a perfume of the undivided universal mind.

It is neither an emotion nor thought. It is a state that fills the mind when the "me" completely ends, ending fragmentation.

We cannot love someone as that implies division and continuity of memory. Continuity must completely end for love to come into being.

Truth

If everything is illusion, what is the truth?

Who knows the truth? The Rig Veda says, "The Most High Seer that is in highest heaven, He knows it – or perchance even He knows not."

Truth is love and compassion. It lives in the effulgence of awareness. It doesn't cast a shadow to know what it is.

A mind that has understood the whole movement of thought becomes extraordinarily quiet, absolutely silent. That silence is the beginning of the new.

Jiddu Krishnamurti